Creative Houses

Coloring Book for Kids

Detailed Architecture Designs, Creative Buildings Patterns For Children

Rachel Mintz

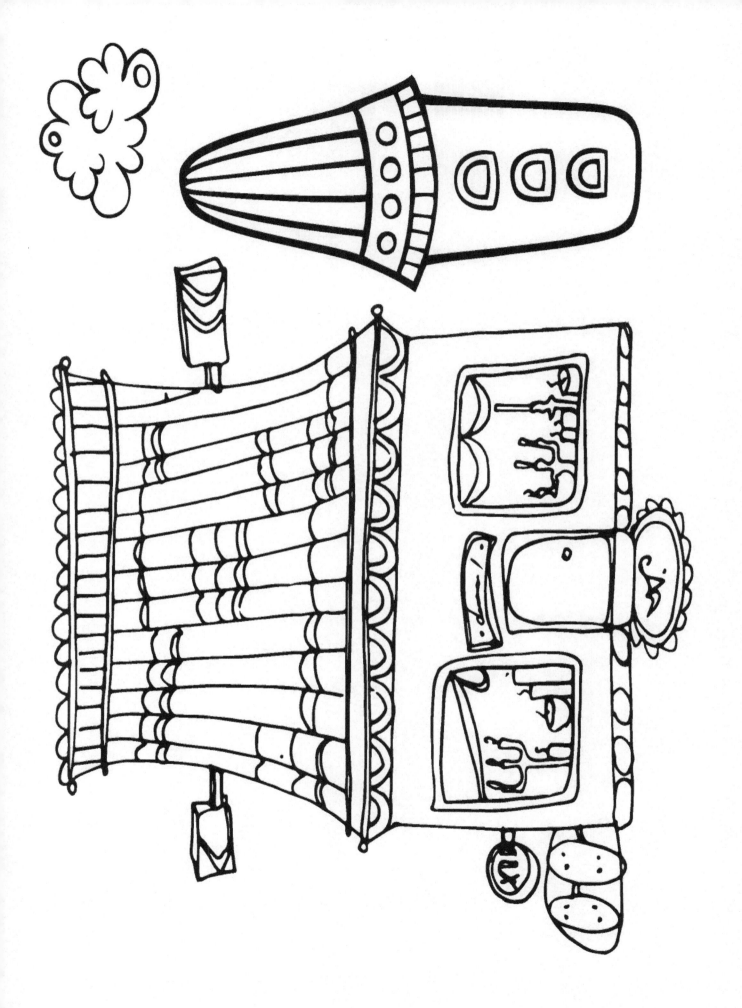

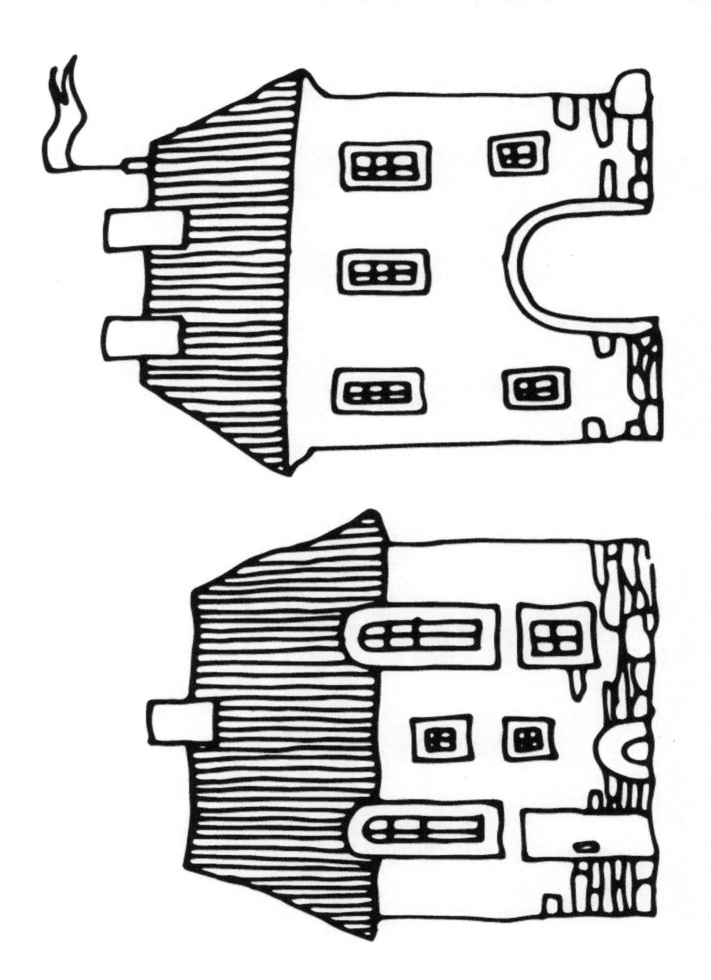

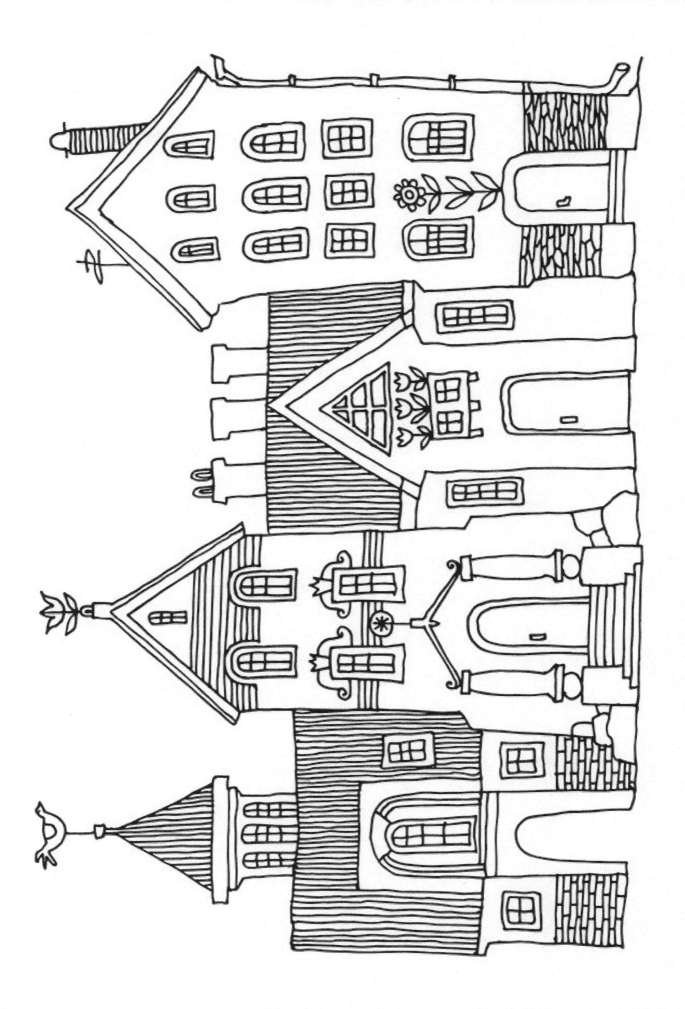

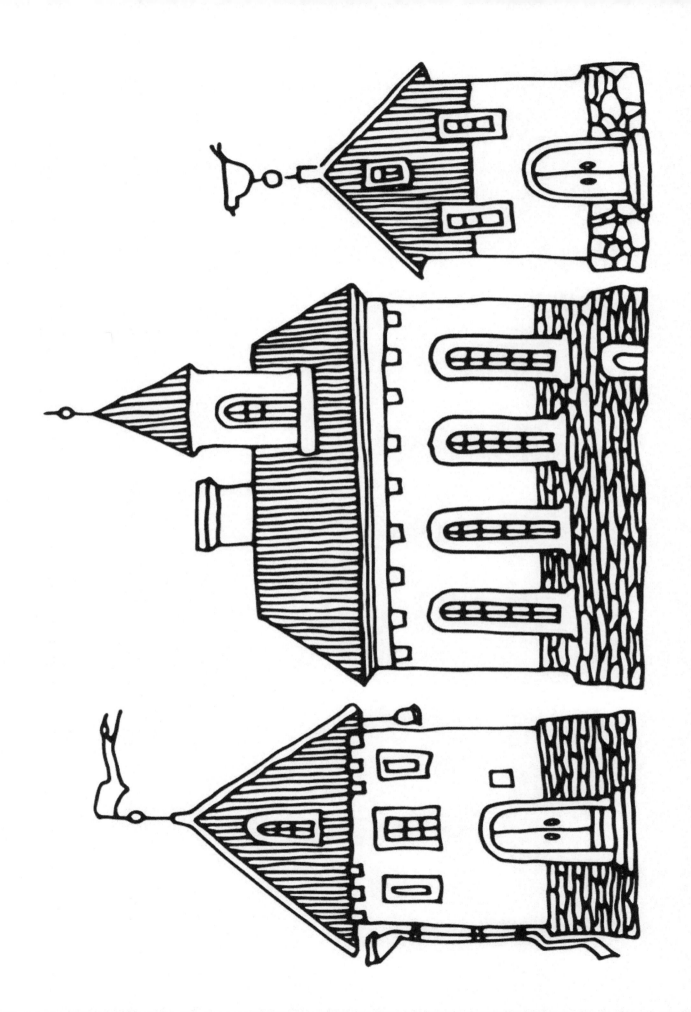

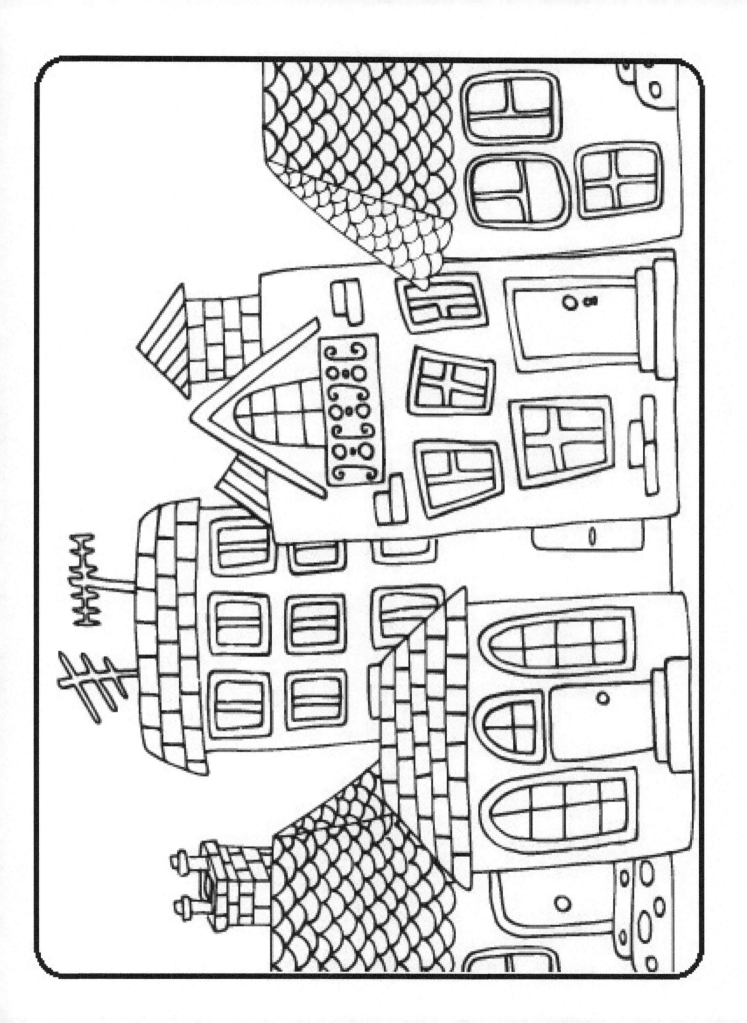

Thank you for coloring with us

Please consider to rate & review

More from our coloring books:

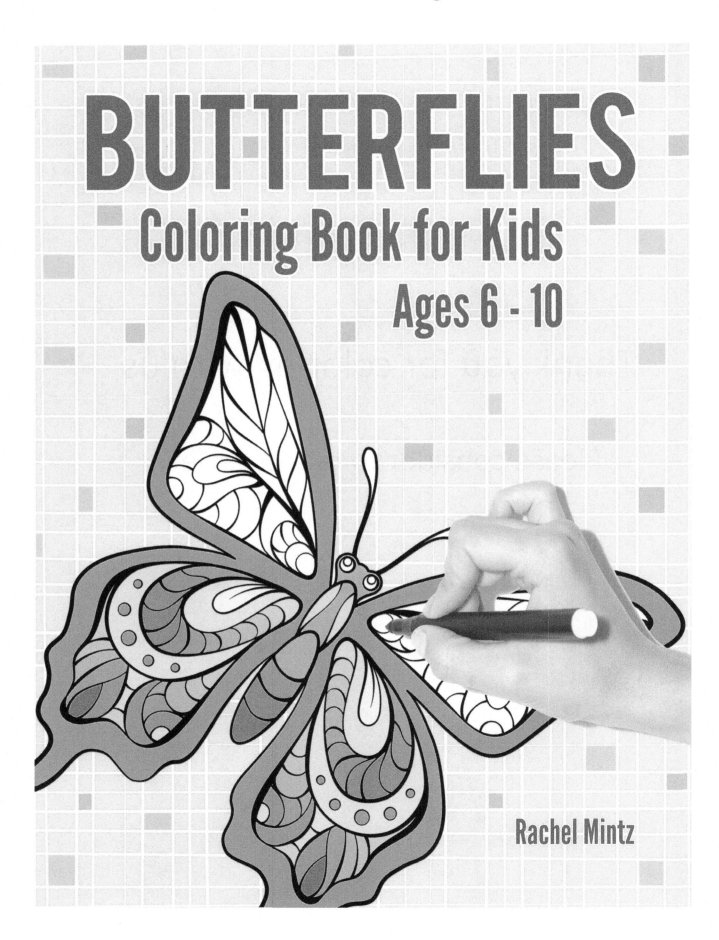

BUTTERFLIES
Coloring Book for Kids
Ages 6 - 10

Rachel Mintz

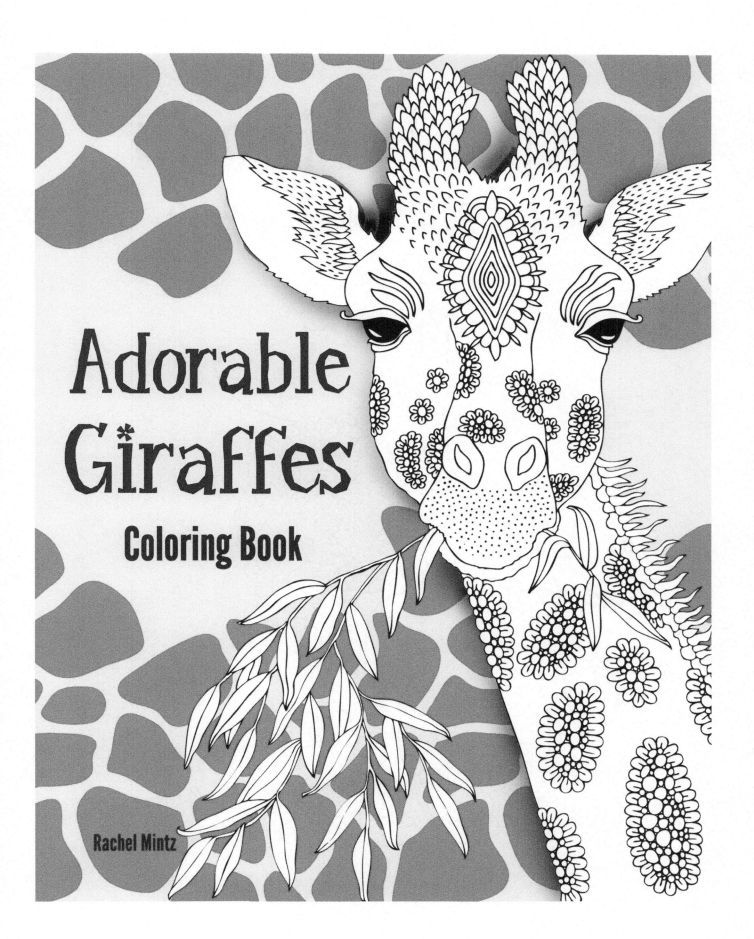

Adorable Giraffes

Coloring Book

Rachel Mintz

Cutie Friends

Doodle Pets Coloring Book

For Kids
Ages 6-10

Rachel Mintz

Join Our Coloring Books VIP Group
Members Get Giveaways, Deep Discount Offers,
Win Prizes – Visit Site To Join (It's Free)

www.ColoringBookHome.com

Thank you for coloring with us

Please consider to rate & review

Made in the USA
Middletown, DE
14 March 2022

62598136R00044